Praise for The Homestretch

If life is a road that leads to God, we better be sure we have the GPS turned on. Steve Gabriel provides an excellent map for the last part of our life's journey. But who wants to think about our last days? It's critical that we do. *The Homestretch* helps us add color, contour, and hope to that important period in our life.

—William Bowman, Former Dean,
Busch School of Business,
The Catholic University of America

This delightful new book by Stephen Gabriel is a gem. Like the lessons in Scripture's *Book of Proverbs*, it's both practical and sublime. It spells out optimistic advice to "life's veterans" for filling their days with God-centered faith, joyful hope, and never-failing love—a perfect gift for grandparents.

—James Stenson, author of
Compass: A Handbook on Parent Leadership

The Homestretch is a wonderful guide for the retirement years, most especially for Catholics. Gabriel covers topics like interior life as developed through daily Mass, prayer, and the Rosary. He addresses new relationships with family members and developing new interests, like mentoring young couples, going on pilgrimages, or teaching religion in the parish. Final chapters deal with suffering and dependency. All the treatments are insightful and, taken together, provide positive support for what will be for many the best period of their life.

—Paul C. Vitz, Professor Emeritus,
Divine Mercy University, and Professor Emeritus,
New York University

The Homestretch

MAKING THE BEST USE OF OUR RETIREMENT YEARS

The Homestretch

MAKING THE BEST USE
OF OUR RETIREMENT YEARS

Stephen Gabriel

Scepter

The Homestretch: Making the Best Use of Our Retirement Years © 2024
Stephen Gabriel

The total or partial reproduction of this book is not permitted, nor its informatic treatment, or the transmission by any forms or by any means, either electronic, mechanical, by photocopy or other methods, without the prior written consent of the copyright owners.

Scripture texts from the New and Old Testament are taken from the Holy Bible, Revised Standard Version Catholic Edition © 1965 and 1966 by the Division of Christian Education of the National Council of Churches of Christ in the United States. All rights reserved. All copyrighted material is used by permission of the copyright owner. No part of it may be reproduced without permission.

Published by Scepter Publishers, Inc.
info@scepterpublishers.org
www.scepterpublishers.org
800-322-8773
New York

All rights reserved.

Cover art by Marinka, Deposit Photos.
Cover by Studio Red Design
Page design and pagination by Rose Design

Print: 978-1-59417-531-2
eBook: 978-1-59417-532-9

Library of Congress Control Number: 2024945293

Printed in the United States of America

*To my brothers and sisters,
all retired and still an important part of my life.*

Contents
ન૭૨

Foreword................................... xi

Preface.................................. xvii

Introduction.............................. xxiii

1. Our Interior Life 1

   Mental Prayer / 2
   Daily Mass / 5
   Reading the New Testament and
      a Spiritual Book / 8
   Praying the Holy Rosary / 11
   Examinations of Conscience / 15
   Confession / 18
   Lukewarmness / 20

2. Apostolate 27

3. Family.................................. 37

   Letters to My Grandkids / 40
   Spending More Time with Siblings / 44
   Enhancing Knowledge of Family History / 47

4. Meaningful Activities 49
   Mentoring Younger People / 49
   Travel / 52
   Continued Learning / 56
   Volunteering / 61

5. Suffering 69
   Why Suffer / 71
   Joy in Suffering / 73
   False Suffering / 74
   Everyday Suffering in the Small and
      the Large / 75
   Temptations and Suffering / 80
   Suffering Is a Mystery / 82

6. Being Dependent on Others............ 85

Concluding Comments.................... 91

Prayer of the Elderly
   by Pope St. John Paul II 93

Appendix: Recommended Readings 95

Foreword

I don't know whether Steve Gabriel ever heard the old joke about retirement—"Getting out of the rat race is swell, but you have to expect less cheese"—but if he did, I imagine he just smiled and said, "I don't know much about rats, but people have a lot to look forward to when they retire, provided they look in the right place."

And what place is the right place to enjoy the consolations of retiring? Not having to get up early every day? Playing more golf perhaps? Visiting places you've always wanted to see? Those things are swell, but Gabriel has something even better in mind.

Declaring that retirees have much to offer and shouldn't "squander" their hard-earned wisdom on non-essentials, this is how he states the aim of *The Homestretch*:

> This book will challenge you to spend your retirement, the final lap of your life, growing closer to God and serving your neighbor.

Steve knows what he's talking about. Holder of a Ph.D. in agricultural economics from the University of Illinois and a government economist before retiring, he has authored a steady stream of books on fatherhood, family life, prayer, grandparenting and apostolate. He and his wife, Peggy, have eight adult children and thirty-eight grandchildren.

As you might expect, then, *The Homestretch* is a highly practical book. It doesn't talk about spirituality as an abstraction but presents it in clear, direct language that not only explains what things like prayer and meditation and apostolate are but shows how to "do" them.

At the very start, under the heading "interior life," he makes it clear that somebody serious about improving his or her relationship with God should begin by establishing a plan of life that sets out in concrete terms "what we plan on doing . . . with regard to our life of prayer"—including when, where, and how. Drawing freely on the spirituality of St. Josemaría Escrivá, he then lists—and explains—the specific items that belong in such a plan, from mental prayer to two kinds of examination of conscience. There are also two different reading lists: one consisting of books helpful in doing mental prayer, the other of tried and tested classics for spiritual reading.

Sound like a lot? Not to worry, Gabriel says.

> We don't need to become an instant saint. We just need to be willing to grow closer to our Savior—struggling to live a plan of life.

You will find surprises here. As you might expect, Steve is a firm advocate of turning to one's guardian angel for assistance in all sorts of situations. But how about not only asking *your* angel to lend a hand (which is what he's there for, after all) but also turning to a *friend's* guardian angel when that seems in order—as, for instance, when you've invited the friend to join you in making a retreat and the response so far has been iffy? Or suppose you're stumped about how to offer encouragement and good advice to a grandchild who lives at a distance and rarely visits. *The Homestretch* suggests writing letters that, without being preachy, give good counsel and communicate real affection. (Gabriel himself has written a book on that subject.)

The conclusion of this small but packed volume deserves reflection:

> Our retirement years can be a rich and rewarding time of life. It will be most rewarding if we approach it with our purpose clearly in view. And that purpose is union with God and service to our neighbor. If our objective, however, is mere self-indulgence, seeking pleasure and so-called self-fulfillment, we are on the track to sadness and disillusionment.

Depending on health, finances, and other circumstances, the specifics of a spiritual program will take into account individual opportunities and needs. But supposing the program is realistic and is followed, the author says, "if we strive to love God and neighbor in concrete ways, our retirement will most certainly be a truly fruitful time in our life."

And Steve Gabriel knows what he's talking about.

—Russell Shaw, author of *Revitalizing Catholicism in America: Nine Tasks for Every Catholic*

Preface

The surge of retirements now taking place as the baby boomer generation leaves the workforce in greater numbers has given rise to many books and articles about avoiding the pitfalls of retirement. Much of the advice provided focuses on finances and how to manage one's nest egg so as not to outlive one's savings. This book is not about retirement finances. Other topics covered in these publications include the best places to live in retirement, interesting places to travel in retirement, and how to live harmoniously with your spouse in retirement. These are all worthy topics that many retirees ought to consider as they plan for this next phase in their lives. But they are not addressed in this book.

The other strand of advice one finds in these publications involves finding meaning and purpose in retirement. This book will certainly focus on finding meaning and purpose in retirement, but not because we suddenly have new meaning and purpose in our lives when we retire. Our meaning and purpose don't change in retirement. The context just changes. We are still children of God seeking sanctity in the middle of the world. We might think of it as pursuing sanctity in a somewhat different setting and with more urgency.

Retirement opens a whole new panorama of opportunities for us. They are opportunities to deepen our friendship with Christ and to serve our fellow man. It may be tempting to think that after some thirty-five to forty years of slogging away in the workforce, retirement is my time for self-indulgence. It's *my* time to do what *I* want to do, the way *I* want to do it.

This book will challenge you to spend your retirement, the final lap of your life, growing closer to God and serving your neighbor. Pope St. John Paul II urges us to see our older years in their proper perspective—that is, as an important segment of our path to eternity.

> There is an urgent need to recover a correct perspective on life as a whole. The correct perspective is that of eternity, for which life at every phase is a meaningful preparation. Old age too has a proper role to play in this process of gradual maturing along the path to eternity. And this process of maturing cannot but benefit the larger society of which the elderly person is a part.[1]

Clearly, we still have much to offer after we've reached retirement, and we mustn't squander the

---

1. John Paul II, *Letter to the Elderly* (October 1, 1999), no. 10. Vatican website: www.vatican.va.

gifts we have received. If we don't think about those gifts and how we might share them with others, the opportunities may slip away. In this book I will offer you ideas for how you might reach out and serve those around you. For Christians, this is how we love one another. We give of ourselves. We sacrifice for those we love, whether it's a grandchild or a disadvantaged family in need of a helping hand.

The foundation of our life of service must be our own interior life, our life of prayer. Growing closer to our Lord gives us the spiritual wherewithal to give to others. As we grow closer to Jesus, we will want nothing more than to draw others closer to him through our apostolic endeavors.

In this book, we'll consider how we can grow in our prayer life and the apostolate. Having more time available for prayer and developing friendships can yield rich dividends, if we take advantage of the opportunity. We'll also touch upon deepening our family relationships, especially those with our grandchildren. We'll try to throw a different perspective on travel and how we might approach that subject as a Christian. As we age, we should try to keep our minds active and take steps to continue learning, especially learning more about our faith. Performing works of mercy is a way of giving back to society and, it turns out, growing closer to God. And finally, we'll take a look at suffering and becoming more dependent on others as we grow older.

I've been retired for a little over six years now. So I'm hardly an expert on retirement. But I really want to do it right. I want most of all to use my time well and to please our Lord in the process. My hope is that this book will help you reach that goal too. The bottom line is that when we've finished running the race, we hear these words of our Lord: "Well done, good and faithful servant; you have been faithful over a little, I will set you over much; enter into the joy of your master" (Mt 25:23).

Introduction

The prospect of retiring is both exciting and concerning. We like the idea of having more time to pursue the things we enjoy most. Yet, retirement is unknown territory. We wonder what we will do with the additional time we now have on our hands. We picture ourselves perfecting our golf swing, traveling to exotic places, and spending more time with the grandkids. We also imagine ourselves picking up some new hobbies like gardening, woodworking, or quilting. Some of us also plan to do some volunteer work at the parish or the local food bank or the homeless shelter. Of course, these would all be perfectly good things to pursue in retirement. But we have to ask ourselves that tough question—what should I be doing during this time of my life?

Many retirees struggle with the loss of a sense of meaning after retirement. This is due, at least partly, to the fact that while working their identity was largely wrapped up in their profession. When they stopped working, they were somewhat adrift. The meaning they derived from their work is now gone. Some are able to find meaning by "giving back" through volunteer work. But this may not be the complete answer.

I would suggest that the most important thing we should be doing during our retirement years is deepening our faith and growing closer to God. Of course, this doesn't preclude doing many of the things we love to do. It does, however, put them into perspective.

If we retire in our sixties or seventies, we retire while in the "homestretch" of our lives. Others have referred to it as the autumn of our lives. We may have many good years ahead of us. Yet, we've already completed at least three-quarters of our lives, even if we live to eighty-five or ninety. But, of course, we can never know when illness will strike or when God will call us to himself.

This should not be considered a morbid thought. It's reality! For a Christian, life does not end with death, it is merely changed. It is healthy to reflect on our mortality. A topic that is frequently presented during spiritual retreats is the last things—death, judgment, heaven, and hell. In his classic book *The Way*, St. Josemaría Escrivá has a section entitled "Last Things." The following is one of the points for reflection: "Have you seen the dead leaves fall in the sad autumn twilight? Thus souls fall each day into eternity. One day, the falling leaf will be you."[1]

Consideration of our death and the afterlife can help us focus our lives and consider what is truly

---

1. Josemaría Escrivá, *The Way* (Princeton, NJ: Scepter, 2002), no. 736.

important. And, of course, the most important thing is our relationship with God. The quality of that relationship will make all the difference. Our relationship with God in this life will determine what our life looks like for eternity.

So, the focus of this book will be on our retirement and how we can be intentional about how we best use our time with our eternity clearly in our sights.

I say that deepening our relationship with God is of paramount importance not because it's important to me or because the Church has said it's important. It's clear that it's of paramount importance because God has told us very clearly that it's the absolute most important thing we can do in our lives.

Our Lord told us that the greatest commandment is "You shall love the Lord your God with all your heart, and with all your soul, and with all your mind, and with all your strength" (Mk 12:30). So, this is not merely a suggestion. It's a commandment, the greatest commandment. But it's a commandment that our Lord wants us to freely embrace. He wants us to freely love him with all of our being.

1

Our Interior Life

For many of us, time was at a premium while we were working. Between our professional responsibilities and the demands of family life, we felt there wasn't a lot of time left over for prayer, study, and deepening our faith. For many of us, this was just an excuse for not giving our prayer life the priority it deserved. Now, however, retirement gives us far more freedom to spend time improving our relationship with God through prayer and study. We really have no excuses now. Fortunately, God is a patient father. And he's given us the time to atone for our sins. You may be wondering, "How do I fulfill this Great Commandment of loving God with all of my being?" Love, as you know, is a choice. It has nothing to do with emotions or feelings. Let us choose to love God the way he wants to be loved. And then go from there.

If we are serious about improving our relationship with God, we have to establish a "plan of life" that will help us do just that. Our plan of life lays out in concrete terms what we plan on doing with regard to our life of prayer. It should be demanding—but, maybe not all at once. Let's consider some of the things that ought to be in our plan of life, keeping in mind that this is how we plan to express our love for our Lord.

Mental Prayer

We can't have a relationship with someone with whom we don't communicate. In fact, we should be striving to have more than a mere relationship with God. What we want is a deep friendship!

Our Interior Life

Friendship requires communication. Jesus said, "No longer do I call you servants, for the servant does not know what his master is doing; but I have called you friends, for all that I have heard from my Father I have made known to you" (Jn 15:15). Jesus has called us friends because he has shared with us the most intimate treasures of his heart. A true friend reciprocates and exposes his heart to his friend.

This is what we do in mental prayer. We pour out our heart to our Lord. We share our deepest longings, our joys and sorrows, our victories and our disappointments. In our prayer we make acts of love and acts of sorrow for our sins. We thank him for all the blessings he has bestowed on us, including the ones of which we are unaware. Of course, our prayer will include petitions. We ask God for favors for us and for our loved ones. We ask him to grant these favors according to his will—not ours.

Our mental prayer should include times of silence, allowing God to talk to us. Needless to say, we will likely not hear the voice of God audibly during this time of silence. But this is a time when our Lord may inspire us in some way. This is just a time to be together. Any married couple who has been married for many years can recall those times when they were with their spouse for hours, maybe during a road trip, and said nothing. They sat in silence, frequently thinking about the same things. That was not wasted time. They relished that time together. So, relish that time with our Lord spent in silence—especially when you can do it before the Blessed Sacrament.

How much time should you spend in mental prayer? A good start would be fifteen minutes in the morning. It would be great if you could add another fifteen minutes with our Lord in the afternoon. Over time, working up to thirty minutes in the morning and thirty minutes in the afternoon would be a good goal. It's important that our time of prayer not be a "hit-or-miss" affair. Let's give it the importance it deserves and choose a time and place for our conversation with our Lord. Of course, we need to be flexible. Things come up in life that require adjustments. It's a good idea, however, to try to anticipate when your schedule will change due to the arrival of guests, travel, or other similar events.

Many people find it helpful to use a book to assist them in their prayer. For example, we can read a few verses of the Gospel or consider an event or scene, reflect on what we read, and talk with our Lord about it. Other books can also be helpful in assisting us in prayer. See the appendix for a list of other useful books.

Daily Mass

The Church teaches us that the Eucharist is the "source and summit of the Christian life."[1] So

---

1. *Catechism of the Catholic Church*, 2nd ed. (Washington, DC: Libreria Editrice Vaticana–United States Conference of Catholic Bishops, 2000), no. 1324.

we have to ask ourselves, "Does my Eucharistic piety reflect this incredible truth?" If not, it's not too late to change and place the Eucharist at the center of our lives. We need to make the effort to ensure that the Eucharist is the source and summit of our lives!

I won't go through an exhaustive explanation of the Mass here, though I encourage you to read up on the Mass in the *Catechism of the Catholic Church* and other good books on the topic. There are two things that I'd like to emphasize here that I hope will convince you that daily Mass is absolutely essential for anyone who is in love with our Lord or who wants to be in love with him. We refer to the Mass as the Holy Sacrifice of the Mass because it is indeed a sacrifice. In fact, it is the re-presentation, in an unbloody manner, of the sacrifice of Jesus on the Cross. When we pray the Mass, we are at Calvary witnessing the sacrifice of Jesus on the Cross. Jesus is not dying again. It's the same sacrifice made present to us at every Mass we attend. God can do this because he is not constrained by space and time.

Catholics believe that the Eucharist is the Body, Blood, soul, and divinity of Jesus Christ. It's not merely a symbol. It's truly the Real Presence of Jesus. We believe that while the bread and wine retain the appearances of bread and wine, their substance is changed. We believe this for one reason and one reason only: because we have Jesus's word for it. Read our Lord's Eucharistic discourse in the sixth chapter of the Gospel of John and then go to the words of Jesus at the Last Supper when he instituted the Eucharist and the priesthood.

"So Jesus said to them, 'Truly, truly, I say to you, unless you eat the flesh of the Son of man and drink his blood, you have no life in you; he who eats my flesh and drinks my blood has eternal life, and I will raise him up at the last day'" (Jn 6:53–54). This was no metaphor. His disciples were horrified by these words and left him in droves. He made it clear to the apostles how this would be done at the

Last Supper, where he said the words that we hear at every Mass during the consecration.

Why would we want to miss out on this incredible source grace and spiritual nourishment? We should be convinced that our Lord instituted this sacrament out of love and because he knew that we need it.

So let's make the Mass a priority for us and attend Holy Mass as often as possible. I know some people in rural areas don't have the Mass available to them every day. That is a shame. In these circumstances maybe you can arrange to have a Communion service on the days that the priest is not available to say Mass. In any event, let's strive to foster a deep love for the Mass and attend as often as possible.

Reading the New Testament and a Spiritual Book

"Ignorance of Scripture is ignorance of Christ," according to St. Jerome. Sacred Scripture is the inspired Word of God. And the New Testament tells us about the life and teaching of Jesus Christ. As followers of Christ, we should have a thirst for more knowledge of our Savior. We should want to enter into every scene of the Gospel and hang on his every word. If we want to foster a friendship with Jesus, we need to be more than just familiar with his teachings. We need to absorb them and make them part of our life.

Spending just, say, five minutes every day prayerfully reading the New Testament should enable us to acquire a good knowledge of Jesus and his teaching over time. I suggest you begin with the Gospel of Matthew and work your way through the entire New Testament, finishing with the Book of Revelation. When you've finished reading Revelation, start over again. Over a lifetime you'll read the New Testament many times, and each time you'll have different insights. The Holy Spirit will inspire you in different ways. After all, each time we reread the New Testament we will have had a whole new set of life experiences under our belt, enabling us to reread Scripture with a new perspective and new insights.

Spiritual reading is also very important for growing closer to our Lord. Spiritual reading may include works on the lives of the saints, Catholic doctrine, or the spiritual life. Reading such books will help us increase our knowledge of God and his Church. Spiritual reading can also help us to pray by providing us with a greater understanding of the spiritual life. It can also provide us with material on which to reflect in our prayer. See the appendix for some recommended books for spiritual reading. Reading from a spiritual book just ten minutes a day can make a huge difference in our spiritual life. It may not seem like much of a commitment, but over the years, if we're faithful to our daily spiritual reading, we'll plow through many good spiritual books and acquire a richer and deeper interior life.

A good place to start with spiritual reading might be to ask your parish priest or another knowledgeable person to recommend a book for you. You might also consider reading the *Catechism of the Catholic Church*, which is a beautifully written explanation of what Catholics believe. It includes many quotes from the Fathers of the Church and other saints as well as foundational Church documents. The *Catechism* is very readable and reading it would serve any Catholic very well.

Praying the Holy Rosary

The Holy Rosary is an ancient form of prayer dating back to at least the thirteenth century. The Rosary begins with the recitation of the Apostles' Creed followed by many Our Fathers, Hail Marys, and Glory Bes. While we try to make these vocal prayers our own throughout the recitation of the Rosary, there is also an important meditative aspect to the Rosary of which some people may not be aware. While we pray these vocal prayers over and over, we meditate on the mystery for that day. The mysteries of the Rosary include all the key moments or events in the lives of Jesus and his Blessed Mother, Mary.

The mysteries of the Rosary are:

Joyful Mysteries (Mondays and Saturdays)

- The Annunciation of the Angel Gabriel to Mary
- The Visitation of Mary to Her Cousin Elizabeth
- The Birth of Our Lord
- The Presentation of the Infant Jesus
- The Finding of the Child Jesus in the Temple

Sorrowful Mysteries (Tuesdays and Fridays)

- The Agony in the Garden
- The Scourging at the Pillar
- The Crowning of Thorns
- The Carrying of the Cross
- The Crucifixion and Death of Our Lord

Glorious Mysteries (Wednesdays and Sundays)

- The Resurrection of Our Lord
- The Ascension of Our Lord into Heaven
- The Descent of the Holy Spirit on the Apostles
- The Assumption of Mary into Heaven
- The Coronation of Mary as Queen of Heaven and Earth

Luminous Mysteries (Thursdays)

- The Baptism of Our Lord
- The Wedding Feast at Cana
- The Proclamation of the Kingdom and the Call to Repentance
- The Transfiguration of Our Lord
- The Institution of the Eucharist

As you can see, the Rosary is rich in meaning and a wonderful source of spiritual content, putting us in touch with the lives of Jesus and Mary in a very profound manner. One way to characterize praying the Rosary is a meditation on the key moments in the lives of Jesus and Mary to the sweet background music of Hail Marys.

Making a commitment to pray the Rosary every day will be a big step toward growing closer to Jesus, and it will please both him and his Blessed Mother immensely. It only takes about fifteen to twenty minutes to pray the Rosary. It's a wonderful prayer to pray as a family. In fact, the Church grants a plenary indulgence to those who pray the family Rosary (under the usual conditions).

We can pray the Rosary anywhere—while driving the car on a road trip, while sitting in the waiting room for a doctor's appointment, or while going for a walk around the neighborhood. The ideal place to pray the Rosary, however, would be somewhere you can effectively meditate and reflect on the mysteries.

Examinations of Conscience

Examinations of conscience are vital to anyone who wishes to make progress in their interior life. St. Josemaría Escrivá pointed out, "Examination of conscience: a daily task. Book-keeping is never neglected by anyone in business. And is there any business worth more than the business of eternal life?"[2] If we are serious about adopting a more demanding life of prayer, we have to keep track of how we are doing. Where are we dropping the ball? What are we doing well? When we identify the areas that need improvement, we can then come up with a plan, maybe with the help of a spiritual advisor, to do better.

There are two kinds of examinations of conscience. Both are essential. The first is the particular exam. The particular exam is used to root out a particular vice or defect that we've identified and that is holding us back in our quest to

---

2. Escrivá, *The Way*, no. 235.

grow closer to our Lord. It could be impatience or sensuality or laziness. We can ask ourselves, for example, Do I tend to lay in bed for another five or ten minutes in the morning after the alarm goes off? Am I looking at websites or other online material that make it difficult to live the virtue of purity—or worse? Do I tend to gossip? Do I waste time on social media? These kinds of vices or defects can prevent us from making the progress we'd like to make in our spiritual life. In our particular exam we identify one vice or defect and attack it aggressively every day. Once a day we reflect on how we have performed with regard to the vice or defect that we are trying to eliminate from our lives.

The general examination of conscience is, well, more general. Once a day, toward the end of the day, we consider how our day has gone with respect to our plan of life and other things. For example, did I skip my morning prayer or the Rosary? Did I lose my temper with a member of my family or a friend? Are there some things I wish I had done better? Did I procrastinate? Also, what went well today? We spend about three minutes examining our conscience at the end of the day and then make a specific resolution for the next day.

The examinations of conscience are not intended to make us scrupulous. We're simply holding ourselves accountable. We've made a commitment to live a particular plan of life and to try to grow in the virtues. We shouldn't be surprised when we fall short from time to time. We are weak and we are sinners struggling up the inclined plane toward holiness. We shouldn't get discouraged. And we shouldn't give up. This is a time for a heavy dose of humility as we ask our Lord for the grace to do better.

An important benefit of doing daily examinations of conscience is that we will gradually grow in self-knowledge. We will also be far better prepared to make a good confession on a regular basis.

Confession

The sacrament of confession is an encounter with Jesus that we should look forward to at least once a month. I say it's an encounter with Jesus because it is Jesus to whom we confess our sins and it is Jesus who forgives us. St. John Paul II said, referring to priests, "Just as at the altar where he celebrates the eucharist and just as in each one of the sacraments, so the priest, as the minister of penance, acts 'in persona Christi.'"[3]

So, in the sacrament of confession the priest acts "in the person of Christ." In a sense, the priest lends his voice to Jesus as he absolves us of our sins.

The sacrament of confession is a wonderful gift that was given to us by Jesus himself. Jesus appeared to his disciples after his resurrection and said, "Receive the Holy Spirit. If you forgive the sins of any, they are forgiven; if you retain the sins

---

3. John Paul II, Apostolic Exhortation *Reconciliation and Penance* (December 2, 1984), no. 29. Vatican website: www.vatican.va.

of any, they are retained." (Jn 20:22–23) Some people tell us that they can confess their sins directly to God. And, of course, they can. And we too can and should bring our sins and failings to our Lord in our prayer and ask him for forgiveness. Nevertheless, it would be the height of presumption for us to decide how we will seek forgiveness of our sins, when Jesus himself has specified that we should avail ourselves of the ministry of his Church through his ordained priests to obtain forgiveness.

Confession is not just for mortal sins, those sins that are grave and separate us from the friendship of God. If we are unfortunate enough to have committed a mortal sin, we should get to the sacrament of confession as soon as possible. Although venial sins and other faults and failings need not be confessed in the sacrament to obtain forgiveness, it is highly recommended that we bring our venial sins to confession, nonetheless. Confessing our venial sins and small acts of selfishness and the like is a wonderful act of humility and enables us to receive the actual graces we need to overcome these failures in the future. We can also benefit from the advice given to us by the priest. In fact, you may consider asking a priest to give you spiritual direction on an ongoing basis. This can be extremely helpful. As the priest gets to know you better and comes to understand your areas of struggle, he can offer you specific advice to help you in your life of prayer.

Lukewarmness

Lukewarmness can beset anyone at any stage in the spiritual life. If our religious fervor and attention to matters of faith and a life of prayer have been lackluster while working, it will be worthwhile considering this spiritual malady as retirees. Now is the time to make some changes and take our spiritual life more seriously. But first, what is lukewarmness?

> The real cause of sadness isn't so much external problems as interior ones—sin of any kind and that special crisis of the theological virtues

called indifference, suffered by the lukewarm soul. A Christian with this sickness loses joy little by little, his happiness of heart slips away almost without his realizing it, and his soul ages.

Now, if one is careless, the image of Christ in the mind becomes darkened and far from the heart. He is neither seen nor heard, and personal contact with him becomes impossible. The interior life little by little becomes a matter of doing things, not loving Someone. Devoid of God, the lukewarm soul attempts to fill the emptiness with things that are not God and do not satisfy. A characteristic sense of discouragement casts a shadow over the whole life of piety.[4]

The onset of lukewarmness is less akin to a light switch and more like a dimmer. It can happen gradually, little by little, as our schedules become more crowded and our minds become more preoccupied. For many of us the question is not whether we are

---

4. Francis Fernandez-Carvajal, *Overcoming Lukewarmnes: Healing Your Soul's Sadness* (New York: Scepter, 2011), p. 18.

utterly lukewarm but rather in what direction we are going. Is the light dimming?

The question shouldn't be "What things am I doing or not doing?" but rather "Who am I loving?" Am I truly loving our Lord? And how am I expressing my love? The bottom line really is simply, "Am I really struggling to improve?"

Some of the symptoms of lukewarmness are:

- Routine. I'm just going through the motions in carrying out my religious duties.
- I tend to do just the bare minimum with respect to my life of faith.
- I lack a real zeal for souls. I don't really care whether my loved ones are in the state of grace. I don't think much about whether they are on the path to heaven.
- I can't remember when I last took a few minutes to read the New Testament.
- It's been quite a long time since my last confession.

- I miss Sunday Mass occasionally, and it doesn't seem to bother me.
- Being comfortable is pretty important to me.
- The last time I remember having a moment of prayer, I was asking for a favor.
- There are one or more venial sins that I'm not willing to give up.

Any one of the conditions above could be a good indication that you are lukewarm or becoming lukewarm. Someone with these symptoms demonstrates very little, if any, love for God.

Why is it important to avoid lukewarmness? Our Lord tells us what he thinks of lukewarmness: "I know your works: you are neither cold nor hot. Would that you were cold or hot! So, because you are lukewarm, and neither cold nor hot, I will spew you out of my mouth" (Rv 3:15–16). Some translations say, "I will vomit you out of my mouth." Nevertheless, the implication is the same. Apparently, Jesus finds lukewarm Christians revolting!

The state of lukewarmness puts us at the risk of committing mortal sin. It places us at risk of separating us from God now and, without repentance, for all eternity.

The point of this discussion of lukewarmness is to alert you to a risk to which many of us are prone. The good news is that we can do something about it. We simply need to make a choice to love our Lord. We don't need to become an instant saint. We just need to be willing to struggle to grow closer to our Savior—struggling to live a plan of life as described above. But we really have to want to love our Lord more deeply. Don't wait for "feelings of love"! Feelings are fleeting. They come and go. Many great saints spent years with arid prayer, even a sense of abandonment by God. Yet, they were great lovers. St. Josemaría tells us how we should love our Lord.

> You tell me, yes, that you want to. Very good: but do you want to as a miser longs for gold, as

a mother loves her child, as a worldling craves for honors, or as a wretched sensualist seeks his pleasure? No? Then, you don't want to.[5]

---

5. Escrivá, *The Way*, no. 316.

2

Apostolate

As Christians, we are followers of Christ. We are his disciples. This is what being Christian means. The Gospels make it very clear that Jesus called his followers to evangelize. It will be worthwhile to consider Jesus's words, that is, his call to us to spread the Good News. Jesus sent seventy disciples to the surrounding towns and villages to prepare them for his arrival (Lk 10:1). Clearly, Jesus wants to involve his followers in the conversion of the world. Undoubtedly, Jesus wants you and me engaged in the evangelization of our society.

"Then he said to his disciples, 'The harvest is plentiful, but the laborers are few; pray therefore the Lord of the harvest to send out laborers into his harvest'" (Mt 9:37–38). Jesus, of course, is speaking of the harvest of souls. There was a great need during those days for disciples to reach out and interact with the many souls who had not heard the message of Jesus. And the need today is also great. We need only take a look around us at all the lost souls who are confused about so many things. Materialism and consumerism have become the new religion. Human sexuality has become distorted and errors are being promoted at the highest levels of government and society. There are many people who just need to talk with someone who has understanding and empathy and who can help them see the truth of who we are as children of God, destined for so much more than this world has to offer. Most of these people will not be reached by priests and nuns. They are your friends, neighbors, and former colleagues. You rub shoulders with them every day. If you don't help them, who will?

Jesus made it clear that his Church's mission is to bring souls to him. After the miraculous catch of fish, he told Peter, "Do not be afraid; henceforth you will be catching men" (Lk 5:10). As disciples of Christ and members of his Church, that is our mission too.

So, what does apostolate look like for a retiree? Basically, it amounts to being a good friend to our friends. Although you may not feel like you're an apostle or that you're very well equipped to be one, living a life of prayer combined with your effort to better understand your faith through spiritual reading and study will position you to help your friends who may be disposed to take a step closer to God but don't know quite how. In your prayer you can ask our Lord to help you to be a better apostle. Ask him for assistance. Ask him to send people your way so you can bring them closer to him.

The apostolate of the ordinary layperson like you and me does not involve doing anything strange like standing on a soap box and preaching to a crowd of strangers. Far from it. Our apostolate should be something very natural. It involves making the effort to widen our circle of friends and then being good friends to them, caring enough about them and their eternal souls to encourage them to pray, attend Holy Mass, go to confession, or make a spiritual retreat with us.

Imagine going to lunch with a friend who you know is a lapsed Catholic. Maybe you learned this about her during a previous conversation and it wasn't the right moment to pursue the matter at that time. Now it's just the two of you and you happen to mention the fact that you're reading an incredible book on the Mass. At this point she might tell you that she hasn't been to Mass in twenty years. Maybe she just fell away due to laziness or maybe there is some issue that caused her to leave the Church. Your conversation then reveals that her issue is the result of some misunderstanding. Maybe you can help her resolve the misunderstanding, or it's possible that you need to do some homework and get a better understanding of the issue yourself. After a few discussions, she notices your nonjudgmental concern for her and she seems willing to view the issue in another light. At some point you might ask her if she'd like to go to confession with you. You might also mention that the priest may be able to address any other concerns she may have.

Being an apostle among your friends is something quite intentional. We are in love with our Lord, and we know how he has changed our life. We want that for our friends too. Nevertheless, we respect their freedom. We're not pushy. Sometimes they will come to us. They know we are faithful Catholics and see our joy. They want that too. It's important that we don't fall into that "It's none of my business" mindset. These are your friends. You care for them. You love them! Their eternity is your business. Woe to us if, at the General Judgment, we meet our friend and she says, "Why didn't you share with me the treasure of the Catholic Faith while we were friends?"

Many of us have friends who are practicing Catholics but may be a bit lukewarm. They go to Sunday Mass, but they rarely go to confession, if at all. They don't have much of a prayer life. Of course, you may not know all this about your friends. But it's a safe bet that many, if not most, of the folks you see at Sunday Mass fall into that category. We can reach out to the people we meet in our parish through the various activities sponsored by the parish. Some parishes provide coffee and donuts after Mass. This can be a great opportunity to meet new people and expand your circle of friends. If you hit it off with someone, exchange contact information and arrange to get together for coffee or lunch. After you get to know him, you can invite him to come with you to a day of recollection or a retreat. There may be a Bible study going on or a men's or women's group that provides an opportunity for prayer and study.

Try to keep up with your former colleagues at work. There may be some with whom you could grow closer now that you are retired. Maybe your professional relationship made it difficult to talk about religious or moral issues. There may be a former subordinate who respects you quite a lot but due to the nature of your relationship you found it difficult to get to know him personally as well as you'd like.

Needless to say, our friendships must be unconditional. Our friendships are not conditioned on how receptive they are to our overtures and promptings. Some friends will be receptive, and some will not. We need to keep in mind that our apostolate is primarily the work of the Holy Spirit. God wants us to collaborate with him in evangelizing our friends. But it's his work. We are just instruments in his hands.

Of course, every interaction with our friends will not and should not involve a heavy conversation about faith or morals. These kinds of conversations will happen naturally and organically. Our goal is just to be friends—no ulterior motives! As our friendships deepen, the focus of our conversations will naturally gravitate toward more important matters. As apostles, we just need to take our cues from our friends. What does he need? What is she looking for? Sometimes we will be asked directly about some matter of faith or morals, and sometimes we just need to read between the lines and take the initiative.

Our prayer and mortification (prayer of the senses) are important ingredients to our apostolate. Without a life of prayer and mortification, we will be ineffective apostles at best. We will simply not have the spiritual wherewithal to bring our friends closer to God. We should pray for our friend and offer a small mortification (like no cream in our coffee) prior to our lunch date with him. It would be a good idea to pray to his guardian angel as well. Doesn't it make sense to round up all the supernatural assistance we can get when evangelizing our friends?

What if your retirement has put you in a position where you have very few friends, if any? Maybe you've downsized and moved into a new neighborhood or even a new state. Try meeting new people in your parish by joining the men's or women's group. Men can join the local Knights of Columbus chapter. Most parishes have Bible study groups or community outreach groups that help the poor in the community. The local community center may offer inexpensive classes on such things as photography or creative writing. If we make the effort, we can certainly meet more people in our community, and some of them may become friends. We don't have to be extroverts to make new friends. We just have to put ourselves in a position where we are around other people, interact, and find some with whom we have something in common.

The bottom line is that we want what is best for our friends, and not just materially, in a worldly way. We are most concerned about the state of their souls. We want them to be happy and filled with joy. And only a deep friendship with Jesus will give them that.

3

Family

One of the most important things many aspiring retirees look forward to in retirement is spending more time with family—especially with grandchildren. Unfortunately, this is made more difficult by the fact that the children of many retirees are separated from them by many miles. Some may live across the country or even in other countries or continents. The newfound time that comes with retirement enables us to visit our children and grandchildren more frequently. We now have the time to make longer trips and maybe even bring the grandkids along on short vacations or field trips.

I know several retirees who have taken on serious childcare duties for their grandchildren. Some care for their grandchildren most of the workday, four or five days a week. Although this is a great help to their children and it's wonderful to be able to spend the time with one's grandkids, it can be rather exhausting interacting with small children all day long. It's for a reason that having and raising children is for the young! Grandparent retirees should think long and hard before agreeing to undertake substantial regular childcare duties for their children. Nevertheless, while caring for your grandchildren, try to take advantage of the situation to be more than mere caregivers. You have much to share with your grandkids. Talk to them about your love of God, pray with them, and help them to grow in the virtues. And we try to do this with simplicity and naturalness.

Watching the grandkids for a weekend or a week to give their parents a break can provide a wonderful service to your children. Plan a field trip or two, like hiking or going to a museum. This will provide an excellent opportunity to bond with the grandkids.

Grandparents have a unique opportunity to provide critical formation to their grandkids. Of course, they need to respect the wishes of their children regarding the formation they provide. But hopefully, the grandparents and their children are on the same page regarding the Faith and other values that they are trying to communicate to the kids.

What formative role do grandparents have, if any? Or is their role merely one of being a friend and companion, going on outings together like fishing, museums, and ice cream shops? Unfortunately, many grandparents find that they have relatively few opportunities to have one-on-one outings, let alone conversations, with their grandchildren due to distance or to the number of grandkids they have. They certainly will take the opportunities to chat with them one-on-one at family gatherings, but those encounters are generally pretty brief and there are usually a number of other grandkids around that they'd like to catch up with as well. If you are able to take your grandchildren out on one-on-one excursions on a regular basis, you are indeed fortunate. What a joy for both you and your grandkids.

So, sadly, the one-on-one time spent with our grandchildren can be pretty limited. No doubt, we could make more of an effort. But, frankly, carving out the time with each of them, given their busy schedules, would be a monumental challenge.

Letters to My Grandkids

So, I asked myself, how could I play a more formative role in their lives? Fortunately, my eight kids are all practicing Catholics and we share the same values and aspirations for their children. So, any formative input I provide to my grandchildren will be reinforcing their efforts and helpful to my children. But, as a grandparent, how can I pull this off? I don't want to be the grandpa who launches into heavy conversations about virtues and the various life issues every time I have an opportunity to talk with my grandkids. I prefer to be—and I think they would prefer that I be—a grandpa who is fun to be with and who shows an interest in them and the things that are important to them. Depending on your situation, you may be able to have occasional serious formative conversations with your grandchildren. I urge you to take advantage of those opportunities. Open your heart to them. Make it a conversation, not a lecture.

Yet, I am deeply concerned about each of my grandchildren and their immortal souls. After a lot of thought and pondering, I decided to write letters to my grandchildren about things that matter—God, the Church, their sexuality, friendship, hardships, work, and so on. In the letters I try to speak to my older grandchildren, those who are about thirteen or older. There are many ways I could have delivered these letters. I could have sent each one of them one letter a month until I covered all the topics that I wanted to discuss with them (there are sixteen topics). But that approach could have been disrupted for one reason or another over the course of sixteen months. And who knows where I would be when the younger ones reached an age when they could appreciate and digest the subject matter contained in the letters? For people who have only a handful of grandchildren, this approach could work well for them, but I thought a different method would be better for me.

I chose to put all sixteen letters in a single volume and bind them as a book. I gave a copy to each of my children for their review and asked whether their younger, junior-high-school-aged kids were ready for its contents. I was particularly concerned about the letter on their sexuality. I printed out enough books for all my grandkids plus a few more for the grandchildren yet to be conceived. I signed each of the books of letters and gave them to each grandchild personally. I told them that each letter was written from my heart. Eventually, I'll sign all the books and give them to their parents for safekeeping for the little ones. I'd like to do this while I still know their names.[1]

How will my book of letters be received by my grandchildren? As the saying goes, "You can lead a horse to water, but you can't make him drink." Each of them will have to decide whether to read the letters and, if they do, whether to take them to heart. For some, they will have little impact on their lives now but they may have more later in life. For others, they may have a profound influence on them and lead to wonderful conversations with me, their parents, or a mentor. Regardless,

---

1. The letters I wrote were published: Stephen Gabriel, *Hope for your Grandchildren: Talking to the Third Generation about What Matters* (New York: Scepter, 2022). An unpublished version of this book was given to my grandchildren.

my hope is that it is clear to them that their grandfather loves them deeply and wants only what is good for them.

Spending More Time with Siblings

We are all growing older. But that's a good thing, right? It certainly beats the alternative! We never know, however, when it might be the last time we see one of our brothers or sisters. Retirement years can be a wonderful time for spending more time with siblings. Making the effort to have one or more family reunions (maybe even just siblings and spouses to keep it simple) can be so very rewarding and enable you and your brothers and sisters to catch up and grow even closer. If your siblings are spread out geographically, find a location that works well for most of you. Maybe some of you can chip in and help the sibling for whom the travel would be a burden. Just figure out a way to make it work. If necessary to avoid discord, you might make a rule that politics is "off limits" during the course of the reunion. But, then again, if your family is the type that thrives on political debate, then have at it. The important thing is that everyone enjoys themselves and grows closer.

All of my five siblings are retired and we're rather spread out geographically. I have a brother in Texas, a sister in Alabama, a brother and a sister in Florida, and a brother living on the eastern shore of Virginia. My wife and I live in northern Virginia. We try to get together once a year for a siblings (and spouses) reunion. So far, we've met in Pensacola, Florida, near my brother's home, and on the eastern shore of Virginia. Our circumstances are changing, so we may be looking for new venues for future reunions: we need to find locales big enough to accommodate all of us. This challenge can take some creativity. We'll be looking for places with fun and interesting things to do and accommodations that won't break the bank.

We are in the early stages of planning a more extended reunion including our children and grandchildren. This will be no small task as we'll be looking for a venue that can accommodate over 100 people. We might need to rent a small island in the Caribbean!

Sadly, it's not unusual for discord to exist in many families. Some family members may not be on speaking terms due to a falling out that may have occurred many years ago. Life is just too short for such a situation to persist. Why not take the initiative and take steps to heal these broken relationships? It may require humility on our part and an apology for our role in the rift and an offer of forgiveness to the other party.

If we've simply fallen out of touch with a family member for whatever reason, now is the time to rectify that situation. Make that phone call or send that email and resolve to reestablish communications. Be sure to pray for your estranged loved one and seek the assistance of his or her guardian angel prior to making that call or sending that email.

Enhancing Knowledge of Family History

It can be a great service to your children, grandchildren, and beyond to do the research and writing that presents aspects of your family history. This sort of activity may not be for everyone, but if you are inclined, it could be a very enriching experience. My sister has done some genealogical research on our family, and I and many of my children have found it to be quite interesting. So far, there are no horse thieves among our ancestors, as far as we know.

I have a friend who wrote a biography of his father. My friend did considerable research, unearthing original documents in various places where his father lived and worked. It includes photographs, copies of documents, and, of course, his commentary on his father's life and how it influenced his own life. It was quite an accomplishment. His book will never be a bestseller, and it was never intended to be. It is, however, a valuable work of history that will be treasured by his family for generations.

4

Meaningful Activities

Though prayer, apostolate, and family should always be at the center of your life, there are other meaningful activities that are especially suitable to the retirement years. These include mentoring, travel, learning, and volunteering.

Mentoring Younger People

After sixty or seventy years of living we've acquired a certain amount of experience and wisdom. We've had our successes and we've had our failures. How many times have we said to ourselves, "I wish I had known that when I was younger"? So, as a retiree, we have a lot we can teach younger people. Maybe we can help them avoid our mistakes. St. John Paul II points to the many instances in the Bible when older people were wonderful examples for the young. He also cites St. Paul's Letter to Titus, which says, "Bid the older men be temperate, serious, sensible, sound in faith, in love, and in steadfastness. Bid the older women likewise to be reverent in behavior, not to be slanderers or slaves to drink; they are to teach what is good, and so train the young women to love their husbands and children." (Ti 2:2–4) In his *Letter to the Elderly*, John Paul states, "Precisely because of their mature experience, the elderly are able to offer young people precious advice and guidance."[1]

We might consider then how we can mentor the younger people in our lives. Certainly, this can

---

1. John Paul II, *Letter to the Elderly*, no. 10.

be done through our conversations with our children and grandchildren. We should be looking for opportunities for passing along our wisdom without preaching. It is important that we offer our advice and guidance in a nonjudgmental manner and only if it is welcome.

Mentoring younger couples can provide a wonderful service. Your parish may have a couples mentoring program with which you can offer to help. If there is no mentoring program in your parish, you might consider starting one—with the blessing of your pastor, of course.

Mentoring young people at the start of their careers can also be a valuable service. Similar programs exist for immigrants who need help with developing résumés and acquiring basic skills that are in demand in the workplace. Our insights and advice can be very helpful to those launching professional careers as well as those just trying to get a foothold in the job market so they can support their family.

Travel

As I was approaching retirement, a question frequently asked me was if I planned to do much traveling in retirement. My answer was always that travel was not a big item in our retirement plans. I know it is for some people. But, for my wife and me, a lot of travel just seemed to be a bit extravagant. Nevertheless, in the six years I've been retired we have traveled to California from our home in Virginia. We spent about a week there and had a marvelous time seeing the sights along Route 1 driving from Santa Barbara to Carmel and then to Napa Valley and back to Muir Woods outside of San Francisco. My wife and I reminisce often about the trip.

We also took an unplanned trip to Rome, Italy, when there arose an opportunity to participate in a short apologetics course there. My wife's brother, a priest working in Rome, was part of the program, so we jumped at the chance. We are now thinking about taking a trip to Maine sometime in the next year or two.

Meaningful Activities 53

So, certainly taking vacations to interesting and beautiful places can be a wonderful change of pace and a way to create some very nice memories for you and your spouse. That said, I think it's important to consider the cost of traveling and whether we are placing too much importance on it. Is that the best way to spend our money? And are our travel plans consistent with living a spirit of poverty? It's a matter of degree and a matter of priorities. Without being scrupulous about it, I think it's just a good idea to consider our travel plans within the context of the bigger picture of our lives as Christians.

Making occasional pilgrimages to shrines and other religious places may be an option to consider. Though we can and should pray while on vacation—we never take a vacation from God and our life of prayer—a pilgrimage can be a time of more intense prayer and the occasion for obtaining many special graces. I made a pilgrimage to the Holy Land since retiring. It was incredible. It was my first time there and, in many ways, it was like drinking from a fire hose. It was just so much to take in. I'd like to return in the next few years, if possible.

You don't necessarily need to travel across the world to make a very meaningful pilgrimage. In North America, for example, there are many wonderful shrines to which one can pilgrimage. Here's a very short list:

- Emmittsburg, Maryland: National Shrine of St. Elizabeth Ann Seton
- Philadelphia, Pennsylvania: National Shrine of St. John Neumann
- Near Green Bay, Wisconsin: Shrine of Our Lady of Good Help
- Washington, DC: National Shrine of the Immaculate Conception
- Auriesville, New York: National Shrine of the North American Martyrs
- Montreal, Quebec, Canada: St. Joseph's Oratory

- Winnipeg, Manitoba, Canada: Bishop Velychkovsky Martyr's Shrine
- Mexico City, Mexico: Shrine of Our Lady of Guadalupe

And, of course, there are many famous shrines in Europe, including Fátima in Portugal, Lourdes in France and Medjugorje in Bosnia and Herzegovina. And in Poland there's the Jasna Góra Monastery in Częstochowa. The image of the Black Madonna of Częstochowa, also known as Our Lady of Częstochowa, is located there.

So, do your research and come up with a pilgrimage plan for the next few years. These could be pilgrimages that you make on your own, or you could join a group pilgrimage. There are plenty of companies that specialize in putting together Catholic pilgrimages. Try to be sure that your pilgrimage makes room for Holy Mass and time for prayer. Frequently, these companies will bring a priest along as chaplain. He'll say Mass for the group and be available to hear confessions.

Continued Learning

Most people, I believe, would like to think that they continue learning throughout their life, even during the retirement years. It's important that we keep our minds active, if for no other reason than to try to keep any cognitive decline at bay. Access to the Internet provides many learning opportunities. Many universities offer online courses that are available to the public. So, if you're interested in enhancing your knowledge of history, economics, or English literature, for example, you can register for a course at a university or another online venue and participate from the comfort of your home.

Retirement is a great time to try to catch up on our reading. If you're like me, you'll never be caught up. There are so many good books available to read. One of the things I've tried to do is begin reading some of the classic works of literature that I had not yet read. Generally, I don't read a lot of fiction, but I figured it's now or never for

Meaningful Activities 57

some of the classics. I still have a long way to go. But at least I've been able to knock off Tolstoy's *War and Peace*.

Most of us can benefit from taking a deeper dive into our Catholic Faith by studying more intensely some aspect of the Faith—theology, apologetics, catechetics, morality. Of course, our daily spiritual reading can help us obtain a deeper understanding of our Faith. But, at just ten to fifteen minutes per day, our spiritual reading affords us only small bites of knowledge at a time. We don't have to become theologians, but we can all stand to improve our knowledge and understanding of various aspects of the Faith. The objective, of course, is to grow in our knowledge of the Faith so that we can love our Lord all the more and be more effective apostles.

I have friends who have gotten graduate degrees in theology during their retirement. If you're inclined to do that, it could certainly be a very rewarding endeavor. Most of us, however, are not likely to make that kind of commitment in time and money unless we plan to begin another career in teaching religion at a Catholic school.

Fortunately, there are a number of other approaches to improving our knowledge of the Faith. We can read some good books that will provide us with a greater knowledge of our Catholic Faith. It is important to get book recommendations from someone we trust. We want to be sure we're reading something that is faithful to the Magisterium (teaching authority of the Church). The Catholic Information Center in Washington, DC, has a Lifetime Reading Plan that lists many good books under the headings Learning the Faith, Living the Faith, and Loving the Faith.[2] This is an excellent resource for identifying good books to read.

There are also several good online sources of lectures and courses that are available free of

---

2. The Lifetime Reading Plan can be found at www.cicdc.org/wp-content/uploads/2021-Lifetime-Reading-Plan-PDF-1.pdf.

charge. For example, you might check out the Institute of Catholic Culture. They have a number of good lectures and courses on a variety of topics. The Formed website is another excellent resource for all kinds of Catholic content, including films, theology courses, e-books, and audio books. Most people can access Formed through their parish subscription. Also, the Thomistic Institute has a video series called *Aquinas 101* that has a number of short videos on the teachings of St. Thomas Aquinas and the *Summa Theologiae*, the sacraments, science and faith, and St. Thomas' five ways of proving the existence of God. Catholic Distance University offers excellent online courses in theology and philosophy. It offers degree programs and certificate programs, and it's possible to audit courses as well.

Podcasts are becoming increasingly popular, and there are many good podcasts on Catholic topics. For example, Ascension Press has the *Bible in a Year* and the *Catechism in a Year* podcast series.

Each episode lasts roughly twenty minutes and they are very well done and feature the popular priest Fr. Mike Schmitz. There are also thirty-minute meditations given by priests of the Opus Dei prelature. You can find these meditations at the St. Josemaría Institute and *Meditations in Manhattan* podcasts. Of course, there are many other Catholic podcasts that may be of interest to you. The nice thing about podcasts is that you can listen to them anywhere—while doing chores around the house, driving the car, or going on walks.

We don't have to pursue our continued learning on our own while the rest of the world is out socializing and enjoying themselves. Consider forming a book club or a theology discussion group with your friends or other members of your parish. I think discussing the *Summa* with a cold beer or a glass of wine would be a perfect pairing.

Volunteering

Many retirees seek to volunteer with organizations that help the less fortunate as a way of giving back to society for all the blessings they've received throughout their life. After all, playing golf, reading, exercising, and visiting with family and friends will only take us so far. If we've been fortunate enough to completely retire without needing to take a job to supplement our income, we've been truly blessed. A normal instinct is to want to give back and try to do something that will help those who are in need in some way.

I think it's important for us to think of this as not merely volunteering but as performing corporal works of mercy. Our Lord made it clear to us that this is not really optional for a Christian.

> Then he will say to those at his left hand, "Depart from me, you cursed, into the eternal fire prepared for the devil and his angels; for I was hungry and you gave me no food, I

was thirsty and you gave me no drink, I was a stranger and you did not welcome me, naked and you did not clothe me, sick and in prison and you did not visit me." Then they also will answer, "Lord, when did we see thee hungry or thirsty or a stranger or naked or sick or in prison, and did not minister to thee?" Then he will answer them, "Truly, I say to you, as you did it not to one of the least of these, you did it not to me." And they will go away into eternal punishment, but the righteous into eternal life." (Mt 25:41–46)

The Church has always had a preferential option for the poor. This, of course, is inspired by Jesus and his love for the poor. We are encouraged to practice both spiritual and corporal works of mercy.

> The *works of mercy* are charitable actions by which we come to the aid of our neighbor in his spiritual and bodily necessities. Instructing,

advising, consoling, comforting are spiritual works of mercy, as are forgiving and bearing wrongs patiently. The corporal works of mercy consist especially in feeding the hungry, sheltering the homeless, clothing the naked, visiting the sick and imprisoned, and burying the dead. Among all these, giving alms to the poor is one of the chief witnesses to fraternal charity: it is also a work of justice pleasing to God. (*Catechism of the Catholic Church*, no. 2447)

Teaching in the religious education program would be a wonderful use of your time in retirement. This spiritual work of mercy could benefit many children. Passing on your love for our Lord and the Catholic Faith could have a profound impact on the children you teach. Some of my friends who are catechists in my parish religious education program have told me that teaching the Faith to children has led them to a deeper faith as they studied and prayed in preparation for teaching the children. No doubt this is a way our Lord has rewarded them for their generosity in caring for the children in their parish.

The difficulty is coming up with a volunteer activity that works well with our other commitments. I began volunteering at a homeless shelter one night per week or so during weeknights. I basically was involved with serving meals and cleaning up afterward. I then accompanied an employee of the shelter until about midnight. This worked well with my schedule until the shelter was closed due to the COVID pandemic. When the shelter opened again after the pandemic, it was only using volunteers on weekends, which didn't fit my schedule. Fortunately, the shelter now uses volunteers from Thursday through Sunday. So, I volunteer at the shelter on Thursday nights, twice a month. In addition, I volunteer at a retreat center, helping in the back office with registrations and other matters. The work is all online and on the phone, and not terribly time consuming. Nevertheless, it's helping

Meaningful Activities 65

an organization that is doing good work and helping many people spiritually in the region.

My sister volunteers for the Society of St. Vincent de Paul, which does wonderful work for the poor. She is involved in many aspects of their work. She answers phones, makes home visits, and helps determine how their organization can help those in need in their community. It also provides a source of spiritual growth for her. She has made a significant commitment of her time to this work and finds that it is drawing her much closer to God.

Many nonprofit charitable organizations can benefit from having retirees on their board of directors. We have a lifetime of experience that we can bring to the management, strategic planning, and fundraising of these charities. I've been serving on the board of the retreat center I mentioned earlier. Part of my responsibilities on the board has been to spearhead various fundraising efforts. I have also served on the boards of directors of nonprofit organizations that provide religious formation to high school teens, college students, and professional men and women.

Take a closer look at the organizations you support financially. Maybe you can provide more hands-on support in some capacity. I was recently asked to join the board of a nonprofit that provides after-school programs and a summer camp for at-risk kids who reside in a neighborhood not far from my home. I have been providing some financial support to the organization, so I happily agreed to help with fundraising and other matters.

The key is to find an organization that you believe in and that provides the flexibility you need to be able to take the time off you need to visit family or for other reasons. Think about how many hours you're willing to commit to a volunteering activity and how invested you want to be. You probably don't want to become indispensable to the organization, but you certainly want to be able to make an important contribution.

Meaningful Activities

Your parish or diocese will likely have opportunities for volunteering. It may be involved in food distribution for the needy or other programs. There may also be a Meals on Wheels program near you. Catholic Charities frequently needs volunteers to help with various programs such as its food bank, teaching English as a second language, or mentoring and assisting the unemployed. Soup kitchens need help serving meals and cleaning up after meals.

Volunteering at your local Catholic grammar school can provide a valuable service. You could possibly be a teacher's aide or playground monitor or there could be some other role you could play at the school.

5

Suffering

Human suffering is a fact of life. And it strikes during all phases of life, young and old. But, for those of us who are older, suffering is a more frequent companion, unwanted though it may be. As we grow older, so do the rest of our family. Our children and grandchildren grow older, and their problems, when they occur, tend to be more serious. It seems that the older people are, the more likely they are to have health problems. I used to think that when my children were married and out of the house, I could breathe a sigh of relief. But no. Instead, my worries just multiplied.

Now, rather than just worrying about my kids, I also worry about their spouses and their kids. And because I love them, when they suffer, I suffer.

Another source of suffering for older people is that all their friends and other family members are getting older. Many of these loved ones are dealing with health problems, some of which are serious matters. And, of course, older folks find that they are going to far more funerals than they did when they were younger. When people we care about are suffering or when we lose a good friend or family member, it's a source of suffering for us as well.

We each have our own personal sources of suffering. We, too, have health issues. Some may be simple aches and pains, and others may be quite serious. We may have financial problems. Despite our efforts to save in preparation for retirement, perhaps our efforts simply fell short and we find ourselves struggling to make ends meet. Maybe there has been a falling out with a loved one that we can't seem to repair despite our efforts. Also, misunderstandings with friends or family members can cause considerable suffering, especially if the misunderstandings persist.

Why Suffer

Pain and suffering are consequences of original sin. They are an integral part of daily life. Fortunately, pain and suffering are compatible with happiness and joy, because it is in them that we encounter the Cross of Christ. In fact, St. Josemaría said, "In this life of ours we must expect the Cross. Those who do not expect the Cross are not Christians, and they will be unable to avoid their own 'cross,' which will drive them to despair."[1]

We need to strive to view our suffering with a supernatural perspective. This will help us see

---

1. Josemaría Escrivá, *The Forge* (New York: Scepter, 2001), no. 763.

our suffering in its full meaning—its redemptive meaning. St. Paul gave us the perspective we need when he said, "Now I rejoice in my sufferings for your sake, and in my flesh I complete what is lacking in Christ's afflictions for the sake of his body, that is, the church" (Col 1:24). Of course, Christ's suffering and death were more than sufficient to redeem all of mankind. But he wants us to unite our suffering with his. When we do so, our suffering can acquire a redemptive quality. Jesus is inviting us to co-redeem, to participate, through our suffering, in the redemption of all the world. St. John Paul II addressed this redemptive quality of human suffering:

> *Each one is also called to share in that suffering* through which the Redemption was accomplished. He is called to share in that suffering through which all human suffering has also been redeemed. In bringing about the Redemption through suffering, Christ *has also raised human suffering to the level of the*

Redemption. Thus each man, in his suffering, can also become a sharer in the redemptive suffering of Christ.[2]

Joy in Suffering

Human suffering is truly mysterious. Yet, with faith, we can see God's fatherly providence. When we suffer, he treats us like he treated his beloved son. We need to try to see suffering as a gift, because it enables us to serve here on earth at least part of the temporal punishment owed due to our sins. St. Vincent de Paul is reported to have said, "If we only knew the precious treasure hidden in infirmities, we would receive them with the same joy with which we receive the greatest benefits, and we would bear them without ever complaining or showing signs of weariness."

---

2. John Paul II, Apostolic Letter on the Christian Meaning of Human Suffering *Salvifici Doloris* (February 11, 1984), no. 19. Vatican website: www.vatican.va.

St. John Paul II addressed the suffering of the elderly and reminded us that God gives us the grace we need during these times:

> When God permits us to suffer because of illness, loneliness or other reasons associated with old age, he always gives us the grace and strength to unite ourselves with greater love to the sacrifice of his Son and to share ever more fully in his plan of salvation. Let us be convinced of this: he is our Father, a Father rich in love and mercy![3]

False Suffering

We should be mindful of false suffering, which can afflict us if we are not careful. Some people suffer needlessly due to self-love, envy, or the fear of losing things they possess, such as health.

---

3. John Paul II, *Letter to the Elderly*, no. 13.

They yearn for well-being at all costs. They lack a true spirit of poverty. These people become sad because of the good fortune of others. They may also be worried about being appreciated. The root of this suffering is pride. If we find that we are sad or unsettled, we should examine our conscience deeply to discover its cause. St. James advises, "Is any one among you suffering? Let him pray" (Jas 5:13). Through our prayer and consultation with a good priest, we can uncover any unjustified suffering we may be enduring.

Everyday Suffering in the Small and the Large

We can be sure suffering will come our way whether we're ready for it or not. Of course, we can never be fully prepared for some kinds of suffering. But, if we're accustomed to dying to ourselves just a bit regarding little things—something called *mortification*—we can be better prepared for dealing with more serious contradictions and suffering. For example, we might consider a simple fast periodically, something similar to the Lenten fast on Ash Wednesday or Good Friday. Or we could delay having a drink of water for a few minutes after a long walk. We can offer these small mortifications for a friend or family member who is experiencing some difficulty. Another good mortification would be to be cheerful and not complain on those days that are particularly hot or cold. We can offer up our discomfort for a loved one in need of special graces.

When we are misunderstood, it's easy for us to feel sorry for ourselves and maybe harbor uncharitable thoughts or feelings toward the guilty party. Let's try to not go there and assume that the misunderstanding is unintentional. Give them the benefit of the doubt. We could reach out to them and try to smooth things over.

When we have a minor illness, we can try not to make too much of it and make an effort to be cheerful. Again, we can offer our illness up for a friend in need. It is said that St. Thérèse of Lisieux, speaking to her novices, remarked, "I always want to see you behaving like a brave soldier who does not complain about his own suffering but takes his comrades' wounds seriously and treats his own as nothing but scratches."[4] Let's try to take the Little Flower's advice to heart and downplay our illnesses while doting on our ailing friends and family.

Sooner or later we all have to face serious suffering in some form. We or a family member are diagnosed with a serious illness. Or a loved one passes away. It could be a spouse, a child, a grandchild, or a friend. These crosses can truly rock our world. They can even be faith-shaking! It can be so difficult to understand why these things happen. Why

---

4. The quote is related by Hans Urs von Balthasar in *Two Sisters in the Spirit*, as quoted in "Therese—Little Flower or Fierce Warrior," Holy Family School of Faith, https://schooloffaith.com/rosary-archive/therese-little-flower-or-fierce-warrior.

does God allow them to happen? He's supposed to be a loving father. And, of course, he is a loving father! We have to believe that everything that happens is for the good. God sees the big picture. He sees the good that can come from our suffering, even though it is totally hidden from us. We can ask God for the grace to embrace these crosses when they come our way and strive to be cheerful and trusting in God's providence.

I have learned a lot about suffering with a supernatural outlook from my daughter, Elena, and her husband, Pat. Their fifth child was born with a terminal genetic disease. John Paul lived for about fourteen months. Elena and Pat suffered tremendously as they struggled to keep their son alive at home with the assistance of nurse's aides. John Paul had a feeding tube and a tracheotomy to enable him to breathe. He had to be cared for twenty-four hours a day. And there were frequent crises that required an emergency change of his tracheostomy tube. It was an emotionally and physically exhausting experience. Yet, Elena and Pat united their suffering to the Cross of Christ and incredible graces flowed from their ordeal. Elena wrote touching and inspiring letters to John Paul that she shared with others on a blog. Many people prayed for Elena, Pat, and John Paul, and benefited from the supernatural journey they were witnessing. Pat's brother and his fellow seminarians referred to my tiny grandson as John Paul the Small.

Elena and Pat now have seven living children and a saint in heaven. Now, some twelve years later, Elena and Pat hang a Christmas stocking with John Paul's name on it and they put notes from family and friends with special intentions in the stocking. Their family still visits his grave every year on the anniversary of his entry into heaven. Their collective ordeal was horrific. Yet, many people grew closer to God as a result. I have a few friends who, from time to time, remind me that they still have John Paul's funeral Mass card pinned to a bulletin board and that they regularly pray to him.

We all know people who have faced serious suffering in a truly supernatural and Christian way. We were edified by their serenity and trust in God. Moreover, it helped us to grow a bit closer to God, just witnessing how they approached their suffering. When it's our turn to embrace the Cross through suffering, let's grasp it tightly and ask for the grace and strength to co-redeem along with our Lord. "You suffer in this present life, which is a dream, a short dream," St. Josemaría writes. "Rejoice, because your Father-God loves you so much, and if you put no obstacles in his way, after this bad dream he will give you a good awakening.[5]

Temptations and Suffering

We all have weaknesses and defects. Maybe we've struggled to overcome our defects all our lives. It's been two steps forward and one step back for years,

---

5. Escrivá, *The Way*, no. 692.

maybe decades. It's just part of the human condition. We have a fallen nature. We are weak. We are prone to sin. Our weakness may be in the area of temperance or sensuality. You may be thinking, I tend to drink too much or eat too much. I try to moderate my drinking or eating. Or, I try to avoid watching unseemly shows or movies on television or online. I fail often—too often. We should believe that God will not allow us to be tempted beyond our ability to resist. But we have to play our part too. We need to strengthen our will through regular mortification. We need to say no to ourselves in small things throughout the day. If we get used to saying no to ourselves in small things, we'll be better able to say no to ourselves regarding more important matters. It's also important to ask our Lord for the strength and the grace to succeed. Bringing your struggles to our Lord in the sacrament of confession is also important. Even if we don't have a mortal sin to confess, we can bring our struggles and small failures to the sacrament and receive the actual grace we need to do better. The priest may also have some good advice for us.

Suffering Is a Mystery

Suffering is certainly a great mystery. It is one of the great mysteries in life. And it only makes sense in light of the Cross of Christ. Suffering only makes sense as redemptive. If suffering is not redemptive, it is just cruelty. Suffering can be the source of great good. It can prompt heroic charity. And besides, we have to keep in mind that life is very short and eternity is never-ending. Years of suffering on earth are but a blink of the eye compared to our eternity in paradise. It can be helpful to try to keep that perspective.

When we see all the suffering in the world, we must remind ourselves that the only real evil in the world is sin!

When we suffer, we must keep in mind that nobody has suffered to the extent that Jesus has

Suffering

suffered. And Jesus is moved by our suffering. We should go to him and his Blessed Mother for strength. Remember how Jesus wept for Lazarus and Martha and Mary. "When Jesus saw her weeping, and the Jews who came with her also weeping, he was deeply moved in spirit and troubled; and he said, 'Where have you laid him?' They said to him, 'Lord, come and see.' Jesus wept" (Jn 11:33–35).

So, we need to strive to take advantage of our suffering and unite it to the Cross of Christ by offering it up for our loved ones and for the conversion of souls.

6

Being Dependent on Others

As we grow older, many of us will become more and more dependent on others. The first step may be relinquishing the car keys because our eyesight and our reflexes have deteriorated enough that it is no longer safe for us to drive. We all know of loved ones or friends who have been very reluctant to give up those car keys because of what that meant for their independence. That day will likely come for us as well. Let's try not to make it difficult for our kids or spouse when that happens. In fact, they would certainly appreciate it if we would take the initiative and turn over the keys on our own to spare them that unpleasant task.

The day may also come when it's not prudent for us to live alone. We all dread that day. Coming up with the solution that is best for us and our family may require a good deal of humility on our part. I know some older people look forward to the prospect of living with their children, though others would prefer an independent or assisted living arrangement. It's important that we take into consideration the financial position of our children when making the decision. If we have limited resources, our kids ought to have an important say in the decision, as their financial well-being may also be a factor.

My mother lived with me and my wife during the last couple years of her life. She sold her house in Pensacola, Florida, and moved in with us in Northern Virginia. I was very pleased to be able to accommodate her and care for her as her health deteriorated. It helped quite a bit that my wife was not working at that time and was able and willing to be her primary caregiver. I had offered our home to her some years before, and as far as I know she never considered another option. She spent some time with a brother in Florida, but most of the time she was with us. It just worked out best given my other siblings' circumstances. She offered to pay us rent, though we really didn't want her to. We relented, however, and accepted her nominal rent payments each month because she wanted it that way and it made her feel better.

I'm not sure how we can prepare for that stage in our lives when we become more dependent on others. Nevertheless, it would seem that those with a childlike dependence on God, a dependence fostered throughout their life, might be better prepared to rely on others in old age. We all need to strive to place our trust in God's providence. He is our Father and he loves us deeply. We may be able to accept this stage of dependence more readily if we take St. Paul's words to heart: "We know that in everything God works for good with those who love him" (Rom 8:28).

When it's our turn to be dependent on others, let's not make it difficult for them. A little humility will go a long way. Accept the help that is offered—accept it graciously. Being cheerful in these circumstances will make things so much easier and more pleasant for everyone. Depending on our health, we can be helpful around the house and offer to do a few chores like cooking, setting the table, or washing the dishes.

It would be nice to take advantage of this time to pass on some family lore to the next generations. Talk to your children and grandchildren about your life and the lessons you learned. Explain to the grandkids about the importance of your life of faith and how it changed everything for you. Pray the Rosary with them. If any of them drive, you can ask them to drive you to church to make a visit to the

Blessed Sacrament. It would be a favor to you, but it would also be very good for them. Don't be shy about asking.

Concluding Comments

୰ଌ

Our retirement years can be a rich and rewarding time of life. It will be most rewarding if we approach it with our purpose clearly in view. And that purpose is union with God and service to our neighbor. If our objective, however, is mere self-indulgence, seeking pleasure and so-called self-fulfillment, we are on the track to sadness and disillusionment. Seeking self can never fully satisfy. In the words of St. Augustine, "My heart is restless until it rests in you." Rather, let's take the advice of St. John Paul II. His wisdom is timeless, and heeding it will serve us well.

These are years to be lived with a sense of trusting abandonment into the hands of God, our provident and merciful Father. It is a time to be used creatively for deepening our spiritual life through more fervent prayer and commitment to the service of our brothers and sisters in charity.[1]

Nevertheless, retirement years will look different for different people depending on our health, our financial position, the community in which we live, and our family situation. But, if we strive to love God and neighbor in concrete ways, our retirement will most certainly be a truly fruitful time in our life.

---

1. John Paul II, *Letter to the Elderly*, no. 16.

Prayer of the Elderly

by Pope St. John Paul II [1]

☙❧

Grant, O Lord of life . . .
that we may savour every season of our lives as a gift
filled with promise for the future.
Grant that we may lovingly accept your will,
and place ourselves each day in your merciful
   hands.
And when the moment of our definitive "passage"
   comes,
grant that we may face it with serenity,
without regret for what we shall leave behind.

---

1. John Paul II, *Letter to the Elderly*, no. 18.

For in meeting you,
after having sought you for so long,
we shall find once more every authentic good
which we have known here on earth,
in the company of all who have gone before us
marked with the sign of faith and hope.
Mary, Mother of pilgrim humanity,
pray for us "now and at the hour of our death."
Keep us ever close to Jesus,
your beloved Son and our brother,
the Lord of life and glory. Amen!

Appendix

Recommended Readings

Books to Assist in Mental Prayer

Bossis, Gabrielle. 2019. *He and I.* Boston: Pauline Books.

Escrivá, Josemaría. 2011. *The Way, Furrow, The Forge.* New York: Scepter.

Fernandez, Francis. 1988–1993. *In Conversation with God: Meditations for Each Day of the Year*, 7 vols. New York: Scepter.

Gabriel, Stephen. 2022. *Alone with Jesus: Praying with the Gospels.* Falls Church, VA: Moorings Press.

Kempis, Thomas à. *The Imitation of Christ.*

Spiritual Reading Books[1]

Benson, Robert Hugh. 1921. *The Friendship of Christ: Exploring the Humanity of Jesus Christ.* New York: Scepter.

Boylan, Eugene. 1943. *Difficulties in Mental Prayer.* Dublin: M. H. Gill and Son.

———. 1953. *This Tremendous Lover.* Westminster, MD: Newman Press.

Cantalamessa, Raniero. 2003. *Come, Creator Spirit.* Collegeville, MN: Liturgical Press.

Casey, Michael. 1995. *Sacred Reading: The Ancient Art of Lectio Divina.* Liguori, MO: Liguori/Triumph.

———. 1996. *Toward God: The Ancient Wisdom of Western Prayer.* Liguori, MO: Liguori.

Caussade, Jean-Pierre de. *Abandonment to Divine Providence.*

Chautard, Jean-Baptiste. 2008 [1946]. *The Soul of the Apostolate.* Rockford, IL: TAN Books.

---

1. This list is adapted from a list compiled by Fr. Paul Scalia, pastor of St. James Catholic Church, Falls Church, Virginia: https://stjamescatholic.org/wp-content/uploads/Spiritual-Reading-List-May2023.pdf.

Appendix: Recommended Readings 97

Ciszek, Walter. 1973. *He Leadeth Me.* New York: Doubleday.

Dubay, Thomas. 1989. *Fire Within: St. Teresa of Avila, St. John of the Cross, and the Gospel, On Prayer.* San Francisco: Ignatius Press.

d'Elbee, Jean. 1974. *I Believe in Love.* Chicago: Franciscan Herald Press.

Escrivá, Josemaría. 2002. *Christ Is Passing By.* New York: Scepter.

Guardini, Romano. 1954. *The Lord.* Chicago: Regnery.

Hildebrand, Dietrich von. 1973. *Transformation in Christ.* Chicago: Franciscan Herald Press.

Hippo, Augustine of. *Confessions.*

Houselander, Caryll. 1944. *The Reed of God.* New York: Sheed and Ward.

Leen, Edward. 1942. *In the Likeness of Christ.* London: Sheed and Ward.

Marmion, Columba. *Christ the Life of the Soul.*

Martinez, Luis M. 1957. *The Sanctifier.* Paterson, NJ: St. Anthony Press.

Montfort, Louis de. *True Devotion to the Blessed Virgin.*

Philippe, Jacques. 2007. *Interior Freedom*. New York: Scepter.

Resurrection, Lawrence of the. *The Practice of the Presence of God*.

Sales, Francis de. *Introduction to the Devout Life*.

St. Mary Magdalene, Gabriel of. 1987 [1964]. *Divine Intimacy*. San Francisco: Ignatius Press.

Scupoli, Lorenzo. 1958. *Spiritual Combat: A Treatise on Peace of Soul*. Westminster, MD: Newman Press.

Sheen, Fulton. 1952. *The World's First Love*. New York: McGraw-Hill.

———. 1958. *Life of Christ*. New York: McGraw-Hill.

Tugwell, Simon. 1980. *The Beatitudes: Soundings in Christian Traditions*. Springfield, IL: Templegate.

———. 1984. *Ways of Imperfection: An Exploration of Christian Spirituality*. Springfield, IL: Templegate.